JOURNEY THROUGH
THE USA

LIZ GOGERLY
&
ROB HUNT

W
FRANKLIN WATTS

Franklin Watts
Published in Great Britain in 2017 by The Watts Publishing Group

Credits
Editor in Chief: John C. Miles
Series Editor: Amy Stephenson
Series Designer: Emma DeBanks
Picture Researcher: Diana Morris

Picture Credits: Alexandrpeers/Dreamstime: 7bcr. American Spirit/Dreamstime: 17t. Tomas del Amo/Dreamstime: 28. archinthamb/Shutterstock: 19t. Valentin Armianu/Dreamstime: 7br, 29b. Laryn Kragt Bakker/Dreamstime: 16. Audreyy Baydu/Dreamstime: 13t. Juan Camilo Bernal/Dreamstime: 25t. Jon Bilous/Dreamstime: 8. Arkad Bojarsinov/ Dreamstime: 5tl, 7lc. Borecay/Dreamstime: 7tl. Brizardh/Dreamstime: 23t. Bob Brookfield/Dreamstime: 11t. Katrina Brown/Dreamstime: 26b. Bsites/Dreamstime: 7cl. Lynn Bystrom/Dreamstime: 15c. Camerashots/Dreamstime: 21c. Kevin Cass/Shutterstock:23br. R.Cavalleri/Dreamstime: 6br. Valentina Chakhlyebova/Dreamstime: 7bca. Engel Ching/ Dreamstime: 7tr, 25c. Ken Cole/Dreamstime: 10c. Jerry Coli/Dreamstime: 11c. Czalewski/Dreamstime: 7tcbr. Cindy J Daley/ Dreamstime: 23bl. Dannyphoto80/Dreamstime: 6bl. Dibrova/Dreamstime: 20. Dibrova/Shutterstock: 11b. Peerajit Ditta-in/ Dreamstime: 7bl. Maria Feklistova/Dreamstime: 12. f11photos/Shutterstock: 22. Fotomark/Dreamstime: 19bl. Funniefarms/ Dreamstime: 6bca. Happidog/Dreamstime: 29t. Brent Hofacher/Shutterstock: 13b. Candy Miller Hopkins/Alamy: 7tc. Isebastian/Dreamstime: 7c. Isselee/Dreamstime: 6tr. Jhanger/Dreamstime: 3, 26-27c. Lakesphotostudio/Dreamstime: 7clb. Robert Lerich/Dreamstime: front cover. Lightningboldt/Dreamstime: 6tl. Lunamarina/Dreamstime: 7bcl, 14, 15t. Minerva Studio/Shutterstock: 5tr. Monkey Business Images/Dreamstime: 5bl. Kateryna Moskalenko/Dreamstime: 6tc. Namolik/ Dreamstime: 24t. NYtumbleweeds/Dreamstime: 7tcbra. Olgany/Dreamstime: 7tlb. Charmaine Paulson/Dreamstime: 6c. Pgangler/Dreamstime: 7cr. Marc Prefontaine/Dreamstime: 1. Rambledon/Dreamstime: 27cr. Random Shots/Dreamstime: 27cl. Anna Ratkovskaya/Dreamstime: 6bc. Roka22/Dreamstime: 18. Francis Roux/Dreamstime: 10b. Julian Rovagnati/ Dreamstime: 6clc. Marco Silva/Dreamstime: 9t. Sipa Press/Rex Features: 17b. Sivitri/Dreamstime: 6cl. Evgeny Skidaanov/ Dreamstime: 7trb. Lee Snider/Dreamstime: 9b. Joe Stone/Dreamstime: 19br. sumikophoto/Dreamstime: 21b. Luis Carlos Torres/Dreamstime: 6cr. Marek Uliasz /Dreamstime: 6tlb. UPPA/Photoshot: 21t. Mirko Vitali/Dreamstime: 24b. Lawrence Weslowski Jr/Dreamstime: 4. Wikimedia Commons: 25b. Winconsinart/Dreamstime: 7tcb. Peter Zurek/Shutterstock: 29c.

Dewey number: 917.3
ISBN: 978 1 4451 3676 9

Printed in China

Franklin Watts
An imprint of
Hachette Children's Group
Part of The Watts Publishing Group
Carmelite House
50 Victoria Embankment
London EC4Y 0DZ

An Hachette UK Company

www.hachette.co.uk
www.franklinwatts.co.uk

CONTENTS

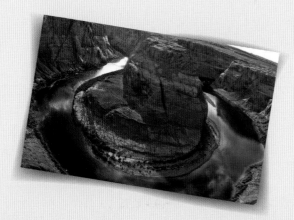

NORTH AMERICA

The United States of America is a huge country in the continent of North America. Over 300 million people live in its 50 states, which cover 9,826,675 square km and nine time zones. You may know that the land of great plains, big cars and Hollywood is named after the Italian explorer, Amerigo Vespucci (1454–1512), and you may think Christopher Columbus (1451–1506) discovered it in 1492. On this journey you will find out many more interesting things about the USA.

Who did discover America?

In truth, Columbus never set foot on mainland North America. He landed in the Bahamas, a group of islands off the tip of Florida, but thought he was in India! After this it was called the 'West Indies'. The true discoverers of the 'New World' were the people that moved there from Asia about 15,000 years earlier. It is an Italian explorer called John Cabot who is usually credited as the first European to set foot on mainland North America in Newfoundland in 1497. However, even he wasn't the first. The Viking, Leif Erikson, beat him there by about 500 years and called it 'Vinland'!

▲ Cold and icy Alaska is the most northerly state in the USA.

What's in a name?

There is still some dispute about how the continent came to be called America. Some people think it may have been named after Richard Amerike, the Bristol merchant who sponsored John Cabot's expedition. If the continent really is named after Amerigo Vespucci, his Italian first name translates into English as Henry. The United States of Henry!

► A tornado is a funnel of violently rotating air that touches the ground. They can be incredibly dangerous and destructive.

Contrasting climates

Because of its large size, the USA has most climate types – the south of Florida and the island of Hawaii are tropical, but the far north of Alaska has a polar climate. The mid-west of the country is known as 'Tornado Alley', because it suffers more of these storms than any other place in the world.

▲ The turkey is a bird that is native to North America. It is a traditional Thanksgiving food.

The first English town

In 1607, three ships carrying English colonists arrived in what is now Virginia and established the first permanent English settlement. They named it Jamestown after the English monarch, James I. The settlers failed to grow enough food and supply ships were late, so hundreds died of starvation. They resorted to eating cats and dogs, and even the remains of their dead! More were killed in deadly clashes with local Native American tribes. Three years after they arrived, only 60 members of the original 490 were still alive. When a supply ship finally arrived, the survivors were so happy that they celebrated with what some people consider to be the first Thanksgiving ceremony. Thanksgiving Day – every fourth Thursday in November – is now a major holiday in the USA. Jamestown eventually flourished when they started growing tobacco.

JOURNEY PLANNER

1

CANADA

Seattle

Olympia

Portland

Helena

Boise

Yellowstone Park

Rocky Mountains

Jackson Hole

Mount Rushm

4

Carson City

Sacramento

5

San Jose

San Francisco

Salt Lake City

Cheyenne

Denver

Las Vegas

Hoover Dam

Grand Canyon

Hollywood
Los Angeles

Calico

Santa Fe

San Diego

Phoenix

El Paso

KEY

——— your route around the USA

- - - - - flight / boat

——— river

——— road

★ capital city

O'ahu

Honolulu

Maui

Mauna Kea

6

Big Island

Pacific Ocean

MEXICO

2

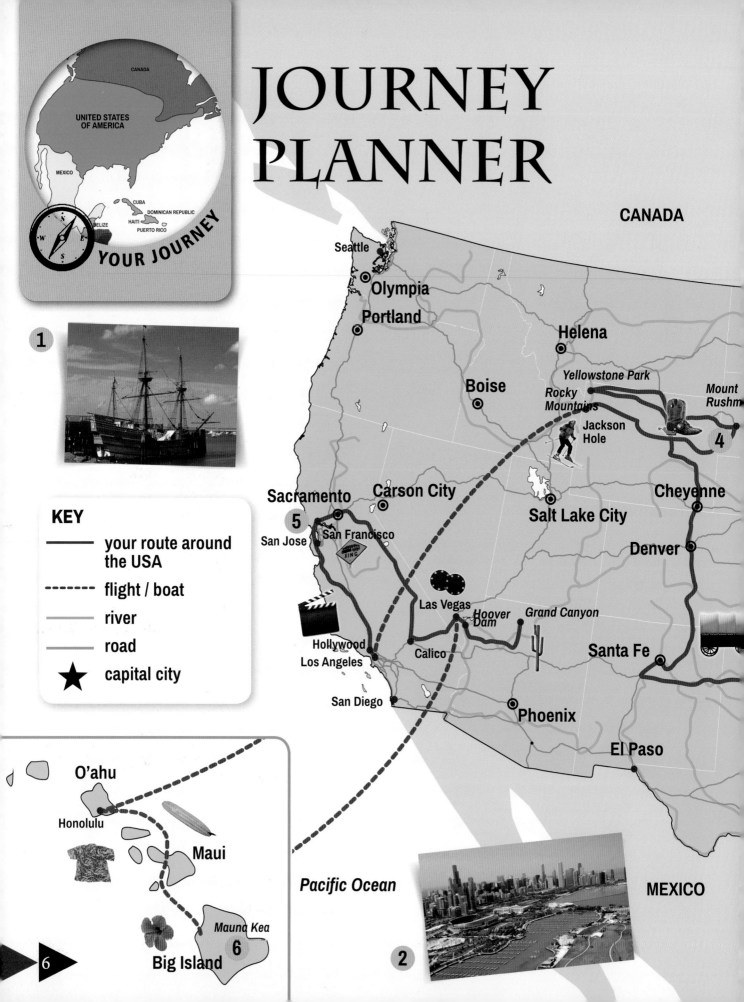

4

5

3

Lake Superior

Lake Huron

Bismarck

Lake Michigan

Lake Ontario
Niagara Falls

Lake Erie

1 Portland

St. Paul

Madison

Lansing

Detroit

Buffalo

Albany

Boston

Plymouth Rock

Pierre

2

Chicago

Harrisburg

New York

Des Moines

Columbus

Philadelphia

Trenton

Lincoln

Indianapolis

Springfield

Charleston

WASHINGTON, DC

Topeka

Frankfort

Richmond

Jamestown

Jefferson City

North Atlantic Ocean

Shenandoah National Park

Nashville

Raleigh

Oklahoma City

Columbia

Memphis

Springer Mountain

Little Rock

Atlanta

Dallas

Montgomery

6

Jackson

Tallahassee

Jacksonville

Baton Rouge

ustin

Houston

New Orleans

Orlando

3

Galveston

San Antonio

Gulf of Mexico

Miami

Key West

7

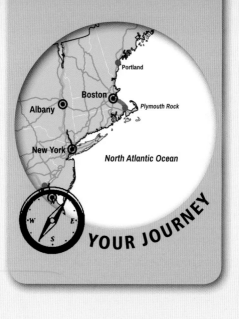

YOUR JOURNEY

HAPPY LANDINGS

Begin your American adventure by flying into Boston Airport. The USA really is the land of the automobile and you'll need to hire several cars on your journey. In Boston you'll visit the site of the famous 'Tea Party' and Plymouth Rock, where the Pilgrim Fathers landed. There's no better car for this trip than a 1952 Plymouth Explorer.

The Boston Tea Party

Founded in 1630, Boston is a major port and one of the oldest and most historically important cities in America. In 1773, angered by a series of British taxes on tea, a group called The Sons of Liberty disguised themselves as Native Americans, boarded three British ships and dumped the cargo of tea into the harbour. The British government responded by closing the port and taking powers away from Boston. This led to protests across many states and resulted in the American Revolutionary War (1775–83), with the USA declaring independence from British rule in 1776. Stay in the Parker House Hotel, where you must try the famous Boston cream pie – a custard and chocolate cake that was invented there in 1856.

▼ Replicas of two ships, the *Eleanor* and the *Beaver* can be seen at the Boston Tea Party Ships and Museum.

BOSTON TEA PARTY ★ SHIPS & MUSEUM

Plymouth Rock

Around 64 km south of Boston is the town of Plymouth, home of the Plymouth Rock. The Rock is supposedly where a ship called the *Mayflower*, carrying the Pilgrim Fathers, landed in 1620. The Pilgrim Fathers were a group of men, women and children who wanted to practise a form of fundamentalist Christianity that was not permitted in England. Today, Christians make up the largest religious group in the USA.

Unlike Jamestown, Plymouth's economy grew because of an agreement with their neighbours, the Wampanoag tribe, who helped them grow crops. The Pilgrims are said to have feasted with their neighbours and some think that this is the first Thanksgiving. Some historians, however, believe Jamestown was first (see page 5).

▲ This stone shelter stands at the spot where the *Mayflower* is believed to have landed.

Modern Boston

Today, Boston is still a busy port, but it is also a bustling, modern and wealthy city. Finance and law are two major industries and it is home to several top universities, including Harvard. Boston is also a cultural centre for the arts such as music and literature.

▲ Built in 1713, the Old State House is one of the oldest buildings in Boston.

Freedom Trail

Boston is packed with historic landmarks, but if you want to find out more about the Revolutionary War then you must walk the Freedom Trail, a 4 km walk through the old city past 16 historic sites. Download a map and discover places like the Old State House (see left), Faneuil Hall, where many revolutionaries gave speeches, and other churches, monuments and houses with relevance to the war and the history of America.

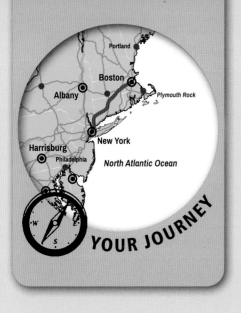

YOUR JOURNEY

NEW YORK, NEW YORK

Grab a famous Greyhound bus from Boston to New York. In 2014 this interstate bus company celebrated its 100th anniversary. For many people it's still a cheap and reliable way to get around this enormous country. When you're in the city, remember to take a yellow taxicab, another great icon of American travel.

'So big they named it twice'

New York City is the USA's biggest city by population, peaking at 8.406 million in 2013. It is also one of the ten most populated cities in the world. Despite its size and importance, New York City is not the capital of New York state. That award goes to the more modest Albany, 209 km north. New York was originally colonised by the Dutch in the early 17th century and, according to legend, the island of Manhattan was bought from the Lenape Native Americans for 24 dollars worth of beads.

You can't buy much for 24 dollars in New York today, but you can at least visit Central Park for free. It's the most visited park in the USA – 25 million tourists visit it every year!

▲ The reservoir in the middle of Central Park last supplied water to the people of Manhattan in 1993.

City highlights

New York has some of the world's most famous landmarks, such as the Statue of Liberty (see below) and the Empire State Building (see right). When the Empire State Building was completed in 1931 it was the tallest building in the world. Reaching 443 m high, the Art Deco tower was a symbol of hope for a nation going through the economic hard times of the Great Depression in the 1930s. Today, business is booming again in modern New York. It's a world centre of commerce and home to the New York Stock Exchange on Wall Street.

Hop on and off the famous subway to see the sights, take a ferry to Staten Island or walk across the East River to Long Island via the Brooklyn Bridge.

The national game

You should definitely check out the national sports of baseball and American football. The first officially recorded baseball game was in 1846 when the New York Knickerbockers lost to the New York Baseball Club. The team's nickname the 'Knicks' was later taken by a basketball team. Today's New York Knicks play at the famous Madison Square Garden.

▲ The New York Yankees are a top American baseball team.

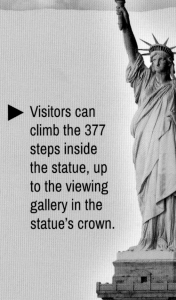

▶ Visitors can climb the 377 steps inside the statue, up to the viewing gallery in the statue's crown.

A message of hope

The Statue of Liberty was given to New York by France in the 1880s as a symbol of freedom. Since then it has been a welcoming sight for the millions of immigrants that have arrived at New York Harbour. The inscription on a plaque inside the base of the statue is an excerpt from a sonnet called 'The New Colossus' by the American poet Emma Lazarus.

'Give me your tired, your poor,
Your huddled masses yearning to breathe free,
The wretched refuse of your teeming shore.
Send these, the homeless, tempest-tossed to me,
I lift my lamp beside the golden door!'

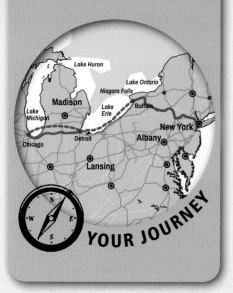

YOUR JOURNEY

THE GREAT LAKES

The best way to travel upstate to visit Niagara Falls and the Great Lakes is to rent a motor home and take your time. On this journey you will experience the huge contrast between the urban environment of New York City and the forests, mountains and lakes of the rest of the state. From there you'll sail to the city of Detroit on Lake Erie and then fly to Chicago, which is on the shore of Lake Michigan.

Niagara Falls

Niagara Falls, on the border of the USA and Canada, are probably the most famous waterfalls in the world. People have crossed them on tightropes and even travelled over them in barrels – some people even survived! The falls are actually where Lake Erie drains into Lake Ontario. These two lakes are part of a system of five lakes, called the Great Lakes. They hold one fifth of the world's fresh water and 95 per cent of the USA's fresh water supply.

After witnessing the majesty of Niagara, make your way down to Buffalo. Pop into the history museum in Buffalo – its most famous exhibit is the gun used to assassinate President William McKinley (1843–1901). From Buffalo, hire a boat to sail across Lake Erie to Detroit. All the way you will have Canada on one side and the USA on the other.

▼ Niagara Falls are made up of three waterfalls. The Horseshoe Falls (far right) are the largest of the three at 57 m high and 790 m wide.

▲ Detroit has a large number of derelict buildings, a legacy of years of economic decline in the city.

Detroit – Motors and Music

Detroit is famous for car manufacturing and earned the nickname Motown – short for 'motor-town'. Giants of the motor industry like Ford Motors and General Motors are still based in the city. Motown was later adopted by the famous record company set up by Berry Gordy in 1959 to promote the music of black artists, such as Stevie Wonder, Marvin Gaye and Michael Jackson. Sadly the motor and other industries have severely declined since the 1950s and today Detroit is one of the poorest cities in the USA.

Chicago

The flight to Chicago from Detroit takes about an hour. Chicago is the third biggest city in the USA with a population of around 2.17 million. These days it is a thriving modern city, which is relatively safe compared to other places in the USA. However, Chicago can't quite shake off its gangster image. In 1919 the government outlawed alcohol, which many people didn't agree with. Chicago-based gangsters, like Al Capone, smuggled it in from nearby Canada to the speakeasies and hidden gin-joints in the city. Different gangs clashed violently with each other and the police to control the illegal trade.

Pick a pizza

Pizza first came to the USA with Italian immigrants after the Second World War (1939–45). It is now one of the most popular foods in the country. In Chicago, sample a deep-pan pizza (see left) and compare it to a New York thin-based pizza – there is a lot of rivalry between the two as each city thinks theirs is the best!

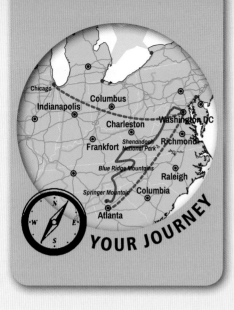

YOUR JOURNEY

CHICAGO TO GEORGIA

A flight from Chicago to Washington, DC the capital of the USA, takes around 2 hours. If you drive, choose a luxurious black Cadillac because the drive takes around 10 hours. Put some flags on the front and people might mistake it for the US President's bulletproof version – nicknamed 'The Beast'!

Capitol City

DC stands for District of Columbia and the area is often referred to as 'the District'. It lies on the borders of Maryland and Virginia, but DC is not in a state, nor is it a state: it is an area devoted solely to governing the country. Washington was chosen to be the nation's capital in 1790 by the first President, George Washington (1732–1799), in an attempt to distance the seat of government from other big cities like New York that had previously acted as the capital city. There is plenty to see here, including the White House where the President lives, and Capitol Hill where the government sits. Make sure you visit the complex of museums at the Smithsonian Institute and the Lincoln Memorial, where many famous political speeches have been made by people such as Martin Luther King, Jr (1929–1968).

▼ The Capitol building is where the US Congress (government) make laws.

▲ Nicknamed the 'Grand Old Ditch', the canal was originaly used to transport coal and other goods.

Appalachian Trail

The next part of your American adventure will be undertaken by foot, but first you will need to cycle 88 km from DC along the disused but still lovely Chesapeake and Ohio Canal. At Harpers Ferry you will meet the halfway point of the Appalachian Trail, a hiking path that runs from the forests of Maine in the north down through 14 states to Springer Mountain, Georgia, in the south. At around 3,500 km, the Appalachian Trail is one of the longest marked paths in the world. You will be hiking the last 1,328 km so it should only take you around a couple of months! Alternatively, you could take a plane and be there in under 2 hours – but you would miss the beautiful Shenandoah National Park and the Blue Ridge Mountains of Virginia.

▲ Black bears are large predators, but are smaller than the brown bears (grizzlies), that live in the north-west of the USA.

Wildlife watch

You will encounter all kinds of beasts on your long hike including white-tailed deer, beavers, moose, ponies and porcupines. In the Shenandoah and Blue Ridge Mountains, be wary of black bears that can be aggressive when they have young. Venomous snakes to keep an eye out for include the rattlesnake and the copperhead, though sightings are rare.

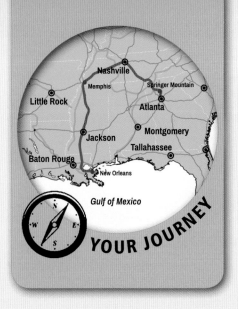

YOUR JOURNEY

GOING DOWN SOUTH

The 'American South' usually refers to the states of the south-east, such as Alabama, Georgia, Louisiana, Mississippi, South Carolina and Tennessee. From Springer Mountain in Georgia, pack up your walking boots and jump into a Chevrolet car to the state capital of Georgia, Atlanta – otherwise known as the 'capital of the south'.

Civil war and civil rights

Atlanta is a big, bustling city with more than 5 million people, a skyline packed with high-rise buildings and an airport that handles more passengers than any other in the world. Founded in 1837, the city grew because of the railroad that linked Atlanta to the Midwest, and transportation is still a main contributor to Atlanta's economy. By the time of the American Civil War (1861–65) it had a population of 10,000, one-fifth of whom were slaves. Many slaves would have worked on cotton plantations but were freed after the war ended. The city is famous for being the birthplace of the civil rights leader Martin Luther King, Jr, who fought for equal social and political rights for black people in the USA. You can visit King's birth home and Ebenezer Baptist Church where he preached.

▶ This metal silhouette of Martin Luther King, Jr stands by the side of Freedom Parkway in Atlanta.

Feel the music

Your car trip around the southern states of America is like a musical odyssey. All kinds of musical genres have their roots here, including blues, bluegrass, country and jazz. Georgia was the birthplace of many major black artists such as Ray Charles and James Brown. Nashville and Memphis in Tennessee are two other music hotspots. Nashville is the home of country music, so a must is a visit to the Grand Ole Opry to hear the latest stars of country music perform. Memphis is famous for Graceland – the home of Elvis Presley, the 'King of Rock 'n' Roll', and Elvis fans from all over the world make a pilgrimage to his former home. Finally, head to New Orleans with all the jazz lovers.

▲ Jazz musicians in New Orleans.

Hurricane Katrina

On 29 August 2005, New Orleans was in the spotlight for other reasons. Hurricane Katrina hit the south to catastrophic effect. An enormous storm surge along the coasts of Mississippi and Louisiana caused extensive flooding, culminating in 80 per cent of New Orleans being underwater (see above). Katrina is the costliest hurricane of all time in America; it took more than 1,800 lives and caused $125 billion of damage.

Deadly storms

Hurricanes are huge storms with rain, thunderstorms and rapidly spinning winds. They form over the warm seas of the tropics, to the east and south of the USA. Hurricane season in the Atlantic is from 1 June to 30 November each year, with most whipping up in July and August. America's most deadly hurricane to date was the Galveston hurricane of 1900 with 8,000 deaths.

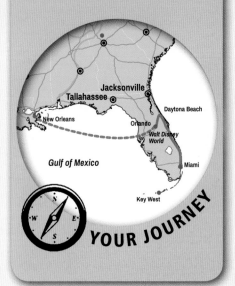

YOUR JOURNEY

FLORIDA – TO THE MOON AND BACK

Catch a plane at New Orleans Louis Armstrong Airport to Orlando International. In less that two hours you'll touch down in Florida, also known as the Sunshine State. The climate here ranges from humid subtropical in the north to tropical savanna in the south. However, it isn't just hot weather and beautiful beaches that have made Florida one of the top tourist destinations in the world.

Walt Disney World

First stop is Walt Disney World, Orlando, so hire a car that fun-loving Americans adore, a Jeep Wrangler. In 2014, Disney World, Orlando was the eighth most popular tourist attraction in the world. The resort was started in 1967, a year after Walt Disney died. He wanted a southerly-located Disney park similar to Disneyland, in California. Today, Disney World covers 110 square km (almost the size of San Francisco) with theme parks like the Magic Kingdom and Epcot®, as well as water parks, golf courses and other recreational centres. The complex has broken the record for employing the most people in one place anywhere in America – currently about 66,000 people.

▼ This railroad-style roller coaster at Disney World looks like a haunted gold-mining town; a nod to America's history of the gold rush and the 'Wild West'.

Outer space

Thrill seekers at Disney World head to the roller coaster ride Space Mountain®. But, if being hurtled around at 56 kph in the dark isn't your idea of space travel, then the Kennedy Space Center at Cape Canaveral is the place for you. Less than a hour from Orlando, you can take a relaxing bus tour to see real launch sites, proper rockets and actual facilities used by NASA. See the control rooms where historic moments in space exploration took place and visit the operations rooms where the ultimate hero of space travel, *Apollo 11* commander Neil Armstrong (1930–2012), suited up for the famous moon landing in 1969.

Which way to the beach?

Florida has 2,170 km of coastline and some of the most famous beaches in the world. At Daytona Beach, take your Jeep for a spin on parts of the sand. Cocoa Beach is the place to go deep-sea fishing or play volleyball, while Miami Beach is perfect for partying. While you're there, check out the colourful Art Deco buildings (see below) and spot some celebrities. Many famous people have lived in this cultural city, including Madonna, Shakira and Gianni Versace. You'll notice the influence of Caribbean culture here too as the island of Cuba is only 370 km away. But Miami is not just fun in the sun, it is also a leading centre for medical research.

▲ An Apollo spacecraft at the Kennedy Space Center.

Out of this world

In the near future, a journey to Florida may include a trip to space. In 2017 the first crewed, commercial launches to the International Space Station are expected to take place from the Kennedy Space Center.

▼ Surfing is another popular activity at Cocoa Beach.

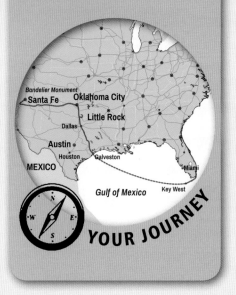

YOUR JOURNEY

TEXAS AND NEW MEXICO

For the next leg of your trip, drive down to Key West and take a boat to Galveston, Texas. Hire a car in Galveston to take you to Dallas, Texas. If money is no object hire a Hennessey Venom GT – a car made in Texas. It is capable of speeds in excess of 400 kph! Be careful though, driving laws in the USA are strict and the speeding fines get higher the faster you go.

'Big D'

Originally inhabited by the Caddo Native Americans, the land where Dallas now lies has changed hands many times over the years. It first became Spanish, then Mexican, then part of the republic of Texas, finally becoming part of the USA in 1845. Much of the city's wealth stems from cattle farming and the discovery of oil here in the 20th century. While you're in Dallas, head to the AT&T Stadium, home of the famous football team, the Dallas Cowboys. A visit to one of Dallas' amazing shopping malls is essential if you're in the market for cool cowboy boots or hats. In recent years, Dallas has caught on with artists and an area called Deep Ellum is buzzing with culture, art and entertainment. It is the largest art neighbourhood in the USA and a must-see for culture vultures.

▼ Reunion Tower or 'The Orb', is a 560 m ball-shaped observation deck and restaurant in Dallas.

Nightmare on Elm Street

Dallas is also unfortunately known as the 'City of Hate'. This is because on 22 November 1963 US President John F Kennedy was assassinated here. A local man called Abraham Zapruder filmed the president's motorcade as it turned into Elm Street (see above). He captured the moment an assassin's bullet ended the 35th President's life. This amateur film footage helped police to catch Lee Harvey Oswald and charge him with Kennedy's murder.

All the way to Santa Fe

From Dallas it's over 1,000 km to Santa Fe in New Mexico. At top speed in the Venom you could do it in under 3 hours but it's probably safer to take a 1.5 hour flight. Santa Fe is at the heart of the old 'Wild West' and a good base to visit Los Alamos where the atomic bomb was secretly developed in 1942. You can also see the Bandelier Monument, an old Native American village with dwellings carved into the soft volcanic rock. Many of the caves are decorated with petroglyphs (carvings).

► The Ancestral Pueblo People were the Native Americans who lived in these caves between 1150 and 1550 CE.

Cowboy Country

In the centre of Dallas is Pioneer Plaza with its epic bronze Cattle Drive sculpture. Built on the site where the cowboys of old used to drive their longhorn cattle north through the city, this is the biggest bronze monument in the world.

▲ There are 49 steers (male cows) in the Cattle Drive sculpture.

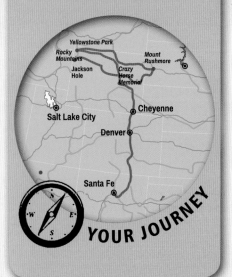

YOUR JOURNEY

WYOMING AND SOUTH DAKOTA

In Santa Fe hire a Winnebago – a luxurious motorhome. Cruise at leisure and in a little over 8 hours you'll arrive in Cheyenne, Wyoming. The next stage of your journey takes you to Yellowstone Park, Mount Rushmore and the Crazy Horse Memorial in neighbouring South Dakota. This is 'Big Sky' country with some difficult terrain, so exploring part of it on horseback is a sensible option. End at Jackson Hole for some skiing in the Rockies.

Dormant to deadly

Let's hope that the Yellowstone super volcano doesn't have a super eruption soon. The volcano has been dormant for many years, with the last super eruption happening about 640,000 years ago. If it did blow then it would probably be the biggest natural disaster ever, and would people all the world.

Yellowstone: A park that pops

Yellowstone became the world's first national park in 1872 and it sits on top of a supervolcano. This means that there is a lot of geothermal energy – heat that is generated and stored inside the earth. There are more geysers in Yellowstone than anywhere else on the planet, but the most famous is 'Old Faithful'. It's called that because it is so predictable – between every half hour to two hours, tens of thousands of litres of hot water burst out of the ground into a spout that can reach heights of over 50 m.

◀ Park visitors stand well back when Old Faithful erupts!

▲ The sculpture was originally meant to show the four presidents from head to waist.

Stone-faced icons

Once you've seen the natural beauty of Yellowstone, head east to South Dakota to the man-made splendour of Mount Rushmore (see above) and the Crazy Horse Memorial (see below). In order to bring tourists to the region, a sculptor was commissioned to carve statues of four presidents; (see above from left to right) Washington, Jefferson, Roosevelt and Lincoln, into the granite face of Mount Rushmore. Work on the mighty sculpture stopped in 1941 and it remains unfinished.

The Crazy Horse Memorial, which celebrates the life of a Native American Chief, is much bigger than Mount Rushmore, but is also unfinished. Saddle up and hire a horse from one of the many ranches in the area for a guided tour of these sights.

Jackson Hole

After all that history it's time for a different activity, so head back to Wyoming for the Rocky Mountains. The Rockies run for more than 4,828 km from Canada all the way down to New Mexico, so there are many excellent places to ski (see below) in this mountainous region. Jackson Hole in the Rocky Mountains, used to be a haven for mountain men and a centre for the fur trade, but now it's known as one of the best places to ski in the USA.

◄ The Crazy Horse Memorial was begun in 1948. Sculpting the granite is such a slow process that no one knows when it will be completed.

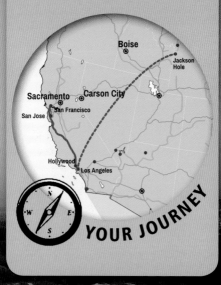

CALIFORNIA DREAMING

You can fly direct to Los Angeles (LA) from Jackson Hole in 2.5 hours. You'll be on the road as you travel from Hollywood to San Francisco and the best car for the job is a classic Ford Thunderbird. One day you may be able to do the journey in a driverless car. California is one of the first states to allow testing of these cars and they could be on the roads soon.

Hollywood

Just a short drive from the airport is Hollywood. It was almost called Figwood because of the fig trees that grew in the area. At the start of the 20th century, when people started to make films, The famous American inventor, Thomas Edison (1847–1931), held all the patents for film-making. He was based on the east coast, so budding film-makers moved west to stop him suing them. With plenty of sunny days Hollywood proved to be ideal for film-making because the early cameras needed strong light to work well. The first studio opened in 1911, and by the 1920s film-making was one of America's largest industries.

▼ Neon signs and palm trees line the famous Hollywood Boulevard.

Star spotting

You know you've made it big in LA if you have a pink star with your name on it in brass on the Hollywood Walk of Fame. This monument stretches along Hollywood Boulevard and onto Vine Street and includes over 2,538 pink stars. Tourists love to have a photograph taken next to their favourite star.

◄ The black and pink sections of each star are made of a material called terrazzo.

San Francisco

Take the coastal route through Big Sur on your way north to San Francisco. The views of the Pacific Ocean are stunning. Be sure to take plenty of warm clothes though. Because it's surrounded by the Pacific on three sides and has hills at its centre, San Francisco has its own micro-climate. This means that temperatures and weather can vary considerably between small distances. At any one time, part of the city can be shivering in a summer fog while a few km away people are soaking up the sun. Hopefully, the fog will clear for you to see the Golden Gate Bridge (see above) – one of the architectural wonders of the modern world.

Earthquake zone

California lies on the San Andreas Fault – the place where the Pacific and North American tectonic plates meet. They rub past each other at a rate of 5 cm per year. Even this slow speed creates an immense build-up of pressure. The release of that pressure causes an earthquake. There are thousands of earthquakes here every year, but only a few are big enough to cause damage. The 1906 earthquake caused up to 3,000 deaths in San Francisco and 80 per cent of the city was damaged. The last really deadly shock was in 1994 when about 60 people died in the Northridge earthquake.

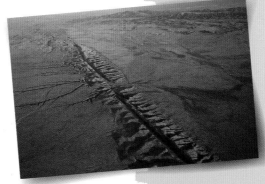

◄ The San Andreas Fault looks like an enormous crack in the earth.

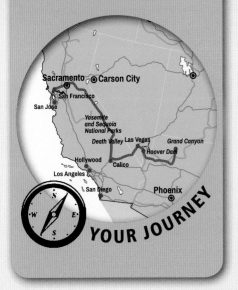

YOUR JOURNEY

NEVADA AND ARIZONA

Jump in California's very own Tesla Model S, the world's most environmentally-friendly electric car. You're off to Calico Ghost Town and the most scenic route is through the national parks of Yosemite, Sequoia and Death Valley. Continue on to Las Vegas as this will be your base to visit the Hoover Dam and the mighty Grand Canyon, which lies just over the state border in Arizona.

▼ The Grand Canyon was formed by the Colorado River slowly eroding rock over millions of years.

▲ Death Valley's 'Racetrack' is actually the bottom of a very flat dry lake. The mud here dries into rough hexagons.

Drive by Death Valley

You better hope that the air conditioning in the Tesla works as you pass through Death Valley in the Mojave Desert. Death Valley is the hottest and driest place in North America. A temperature of 56.7°C was recorded in July 1913 at Furnace Creek, which is believed to be the hottest temperature recorded anywhere on Earth, ever!

Gold, silver and Calico Ghost Town

California is famous for the 1848 gold rush, when the discovery of gold in hills and rivers brought thousands of people out west to try and seek their fortunes. The town of Calico was actually a silver mining town (the gold towns were further north) and a visit gives you an insight into how mining communities lived. Aside from five original buildings, the site is largely a reconstruction. Most of the original houses were destroyed after its abandonment in 1907, but you can visit the original mine and see how the silver was extracted.

▼ The Calico Mountains surround the Calico Ghost Town.

Las Vegas

Las Vegas is famous for its casinos and is often called 'the gambling capital of the world'. It was originally part of Mexico and its name means 'the Meadows', because it was an unusually green part of a rather arid landscape. It became part of the USA in 1847 after the USA invaded Mexico. You won't need to worry about finding a bed for the night as Las Vegas has some of the biggest hotels in the world. These hotels are like mini cities – each has shops, bars, restaurants and casinos and they all compete to attract gamblers and tourists who will spend money in the casinos and pay to watch the spectacualar shows.

▼ This famous neon sign greets visitors to Las Vegas as they approach from the south.

Grand Canyon and the Hoover Dam

The best way to see the natural wonder of the Grand Canyon and the man-made grandeur of the Hoover Dam is by helicopter from Las Vegas. Fly over the Colorado River and the deep, gorges made of over 40 layers of red-coloured sedimentary rock (see main picture). The dam was completed in 1938 to stop flooding and to provide hydroelectric power. It lies on the border of Nevada and Arizona, and on the border between the Pacific and Mountain time zones. This means as you cross the dam into Arizona you jump forward an hour in time!

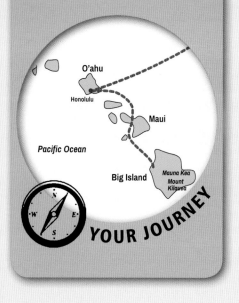

YOUR JOURNEY

HAWAII

A flight from Las Vegas to Hawaii will cover over 4,000 km and take about 7 hours. The 50th state to join the Union is actually hundreds of volcanic islands in the middle of the Pacific Ocean. There are eight main islands, and the biggest is also called Hawaii (or 'Big Island' to avoid confusion). Catch a ferry between islands and cycle around each island by bike, if your legs are strong enough for the steep volcanic hills!

Honolulu

You will land at Honolulu on the island of O'ahu. This is the birthplace of Barack Obama, the 44th US President and the first President with African heritage. Honolulu is a major tourist destination on the island and is where you will find Waikiki Beach – a great spot to surf and scuba dive. Expert surfers may get more of an adrenaline rush on the north of the island at Banzai Pipeline, a beach that produces perfect tubular waves to surf along. It is the large underwater coral reef that helps create the massive waves. A visit to Pearl Harbour is a must for history buffs. In 1941 the Japanese Navy attacked the US fleet in the harbour, which resulted in the USA entering the Second World War.

▼ Hotels line the golden sands of Waikiki Beach.

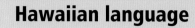

Hawaiian language

The official languages of the state are English and Hawaiian. Hawaiian words that have crossed over into English include; ukulele (a guitar-like musical instrument), hula (a dance), aloha (a greeting) and kahuna (a priest).

Maui

Next up is Maui, one of the best places in the world for whalewatching, as many of these gentle giants migrate here to breed. Maui is classed as one of the best islands in the world because of its beautiful beaches and ease of access to activities like snorkelling, surfing and wind-surfing. However, not everyone on the island is happy about this, because they feel the island is being over-developed for tourism.

◀ Humpback whales can be seen near Maui between November and May.

'Big Island' - Hawaii

The island called Hawaii is a great place to get up close and personal with one of the world's most active volcanoes, Mount Kilauea. Don't panic, it is also one of the most predictable. If you're lucky you may be able to see molten rock actually flow into the sea and create new land.

Hawaii is a laid back and wonderful place to end your USA journey. Spend your last night on the slopes of Mauna Kea, watching the sun go down. Mauna Kea is a dormant volcano but it is also the world's tallest (not highest) mountain. Mount Everest may be higher above sea level at 8,848 m, but Mauna Kea is about 1,000 m taller from its underwater base to its peak. Plus once the sun is down, you're in the best place on Earth to gaze at the stars as the atmosphere is so clear. There are several observatories on top and you can drive up to the visitor centre to see the spectacular night sky.

▲ The sea boils where hot lava from Mount Kilauea enters it.

▶ The 12 telescopes on top of Mauna Kea are some of the highest observatories in the world.

GLOSSARY

American Revolutionary War
A war between Great Britain and 13 North American colonies that wanted to be free from British rule.

Amerigo Vespucci
Vespucci was a key figure in proving that South America was not a part of Asia. However, there is controversy over exactly when Vespucci landed in South America. Some accounts state that he arrived in Venezuela in 1497, a year before Christopher Columbus.

Art Deco
A highly colourful and geometric design style of the 1920s–1940s.

assassinate
To murder an important person, often for political or religious reasons.

bluegrass
Country music performed with acoustic stringed instruments such as guitars, banjos with close vocal harmonies.

canyon
A deep gorge made by a river over a very long time period.

civil rights
The rights of people to political and social freedom. Black and Native American people in America were often denied their civil rights. The Civil Rights Movement aimed to change this.

civil war
A war between citizens of a country. The American Civil War was fought between the Union (states that wanted to remain in a nation ruled by one government) and the Confederacy (a group of states that wanted to separate from the Union). One key difference between the two sides was that slavery was legal in the Confederacy states. The government wanted to abolish slavery, but the states in the Confederacy didn't, which triggered the American Civil War.

colonist
A person who settles in a colony. A colony is a place in one country that is ruled from another country.

commission
An instruction for someone to do or make something, such as a sculpture.

dormant
A volcano that is temporarily inactive.

geyser
A spring of hot water that boils underground. The boiling water causes water and steam to shoot out of a vent at the surface at various intervals.

grandeur
Splendour or impressiveness.

Great Depression
A worldwide economic depression that lasted from the stock market crash of 1929 to the late 1930s. Millions of Americans (and people around the world) were plunged into unemployment and poverty as a result.

Harvard
One of eight 'Ivy League' universities, which are among the most prestigious universities in the world.

humid
Lots of moisture in the atmosphere.

hydroelectric
Generating electricity by water power.

independence
Being free from the control of others.

interstate
Travel between states.

immigrant
A person who comes to live in a different country.

merchant
Someone who sells something.

migrate
To move from one place to another.

motorcade
A procession of vehicles, usually to escort an important person.

NASA
The National Aeronautics and Space Administration, The US government's space agency, which conducts research and missions into space.

observatory
A building that houses a powerful telescope to examine the stars.

odyssey
A long, and often eventful journey.

patent
A licence that gives the owner the right to make, use or sell an invention.

pilgrimage
A long journey, usually undertaken for religious purposes.

plantation
A large estate where crops are looked after by people who live on the property.

recreational
Something done for fun or enjoyment.

reservoir
A large lake used as a source of water.

sedimentary rock
Layers of rock that have been deposited by water over many millions of years.

settlement
A place where people settle and live for the first time.

sonnet
A poem that has fourteen lines and usually ten syllables per line.

speakeasy
A place that sold alcohol illegally.

storm surge
A large rise of sea levels due to heavy storms.

tectonic plates
The separate plates that make up the crust of the Earth and move slowly over long periods of time.

tropics
The warm regions of the Earth surrounding the Equator.

Wild West
The lawless towns in the west of the country at the time when American settlers were gradually moving further west.

BOOKS TO READ

Countries in Our World: USA by Lisa Klobuchar (Franklin Watts 2012)

DK Eyewitness Travel Guide: USA (DK Eyewitness Travel, 2015)

Lonely Planet:USA (Travel Guide) (Lonely Planet, 2014)

Looking at Countries: The USA by Kathleen Pohl (Franklin Watts, 2011)

Not For Parents USA: Everything You Ever Wanted to Know (Lonely Planet Not for Parents, 2013)

The Real: USA by Jackson Teller (Franklin Watts, 2015)

The Rough Guide to the USA (Rough Guides, 2014)

National Geographic Kids: United States Atlas (National Geographic, 2012)

The USA (Horrible Histories Special) by Terry Deary (Scholastic, 2010)

WEBSITES

Check out YouTube for films by other travellers to USA. As well as taking a look at the sights and sounds of many of the places mentioned in this book, there are travel tips and the top places to visit.

A good place to start is the USA Travel Guide by Expoza, which is an informative guide to the nation and its fascinating history, it's also a great way to see the sights before even setting foot in the country:

https://www.youtube.com/watch?v=fHjZD39RL5Q

The Discover America website is packed full of practical advice for travel as well as information about all the major tourist and not-so touristy destinations. The website has fabulous photographs and it will help you plan your perfect trip:

http://www.discoveramerica.com/

As well as books, Lonely Planet has inspirational, informative websites devoted to travel. It is full of useful ideas and essential information for planning a trip to the USA:

http://www.lonelyplanet.com/usa/places

Rough Guide also have a great website which will help you plan where to go, what to do, how to get around and practical info for your trip to the US. It has some great itineraries that you can compare to the one in this book:

http://www.roughguides.com/destinations/north-america/usa/

Note to parents and teachers:
Every effort has been made by the Publishers to ensure that the websites in this book are suitable for children, that they are of the highest educational value, and that they contain no inappropriate or offensive material. However, because of the nature of the Internet, it is impossible to guarantee that the contents of these sites will not be altered. We strongly advise that Internet access is supervised by a responsible adult.

INDEX